The Pleasures of Eating:

Reflections on Food

The Pleasures of Eating:
Reflections on Food

Edited by Erin Conley

BARNES
&NOBLE
BOOKS
NEW YORK

Compilation copyright © 2003 by Barnes & Noble, Inc.

2003 Barnes & Noble Books

ISBN 0-7607-4062-3

Printed and bound in the United States of America

M 9 8 7 6 5 4 3 2 1

"One of the very nicest things about life is the way we must regularly stop whatever it is we are doing and devote our attention to eating."

—Luciano Pavarotti, opera singer

LIKE MOST OF YOU PICKING UP THIS BOOK, I LOVE GOOD food—and, as my love handles will attest, I love to eat! For me, food has always been more than sustenance. It has been an adventure, a pleasure, a social crutch, a comfort, and (as this collection of quotes confirms) an inspiration. But most of all it has been a way to bond with those I love.

Oddly enough, though, other than Thanksgiving, I don't have many fond memories of gathering round the table for a family meal. As a single working parent, my mom didn't really seem to relish the idea of cooking after a long day at the office. So we went out to eat. A lot. Sometimes up to four nights a week. We were regulars at El Lugar (my favorite), Pepper Tree Lane, and the Ivy House. We ate well and ordered creatively to cut costs—often splitting a dish. Dinner out was always my favorite part of the day.

Maybe that's why I never learned to cook. Don't get me wrong; I appreciate a good home cooked meal just as much as the next foodie. I also am in awe of how much pleasure good friends and (even a few) family members get from making a great meal for others to enjoy. For many it's a labor of love, an art, a calling. Sometimes it even makes me want to take a cooking class.

But these days, I just don't have to. I'm living a culinary dream in San Francisco (a city known for its fine dining), milking it for all its gourmet glory. As writer Charles Pierre Monselet puts it so delightfully, "Gastronomy has been the joy of all peoples through the ages. It produces beauty and wit and goes hand in hand with goodness of heart and a consideration of others." All the eloquence in this book certainly attests to that. Hope you enjoy it… just after a really nice meal.

–*Erin*

Comfort Food

Laughter is brightest where food is best.

—Irish proverb

One of the very nicest things about life is the way we must regularly stop whatever it is we are doing and devote our attention to eating.

—Luciano Pavarotti, opera singer

Nothing would be more tiresome than eating and drinking if God had not made them a pleasure as well as a necessity.

—Voltaire, philosopher and writer

To make people who have no appetite eat, to make the wit of those who have it sparkle, to enable those who want these qualities to find them—this is the supreme science of a gastronome-host.

—Lucien Tendret, lawyer and gastronome

Gastronomy has been the joy of all peoples through the ages. It produces beauty and wit and goes hand in hand with goodness of heart and a consideration of others.

—CHARLES PIERRE MONSELET, writer

The gentle art of gastronomy is a friendly one. It hurdles the language barrier, makes friends among civilized people, and warms the heart.

—SAMUEL CHAMBERLAIN, artist

Food to a large extent is what holds a society together, and eating is closely linked to deep spiritual experiences.

—PETER FARB AND GEORGE ARMELAGOS, coauthors,
Consuming Passions: The Anthropology of Eating

[Bread baking is] one of those almost hypnotic businesses, like a dance from some ancient ceremony. It leaves you filled with one of the world's sweetest smells…there is no chiropractic treatment, no yoga exercise, no hour of meditation in a music-throbbing chapel, that will leave you emptier of bad thoughts than this homely ceremony of making bread.

—M. F. K. FISHER, food writer

Before I was born, my mother was in great agony of spirit and in a tragic situation. She could take no food except iced oysters and champagne. If people ask me when I began to dance, I reply, "In my mother's womb, probably as a result of the oysters and champagne—the food of Aphrodite."

—ISADORA DUNCAN, dancer

A crust eaten in peace is better than a banquet partaken in anxiety.

—AESOP, Greek fabulist

And every day when I've been good, I get an orange after food.

—ROBERT LOUIS STEVENSON, writer

I know the look of an apple that is roasting and sizzling on the hearth on a winter's evening, and I know the comfort that comes of eating it hot, along with some sugar and a drench of cream...I know how the nuts taken in conjunction with winter apples, cider, and doughnuts make old people's tales and old jokes sound fresh and crisp and enchanting.

—MARK TWAIN, humorist and writer

And do as adversaries do in law—strive mightily, but eat and drink as friends.

—WILLIAM SHAKESPEARE,
playwright, *The Taming of the Shrew*

Eating is not merely a material pleasure. Eating well gives a spectacular joy to life and contributes immensely to goodwill and happy companionship. It is of great importance to the morale.

—ELSA SCHIAPARELLI, designer

When we lose, I eat. When we win, I eat. I also eat when we're rained out.

—TOMMY LASORDA, baseball manager

Tapioca is the teddy bear of desserts, an edible security blanket.

—JANE AND MICHAEL STERN, writers

7

Do you have a kinder, more adaptable friend in the food world than soup?

—MISS MANNERS (A.K.A. JUDITH MARTIN),
etiquette expert and writer

Cake and pie and bread are dream catchers for me. German chocolate and Lady Baltimore are black-market drugs so rich with inaccurate sensations of maternal comfort and infantile security they take my breath away.

—SALLIE TISDALE, editor and writer

All happiness depends on a leisurely breakfast.

—JOHN GUNTHER, journalist

The secret to staying young is to live honestly, eat slowly, and lie about your age.

—LUCILLE BALL, comedienne and actress

The first thing I remember liking that liked me back was food.

—VALERIE HARPER, actress, *Rhoda*

All's well that ends with a good meal.

—ARNOLD LOBEL, illustrator and children's writer

Food for Thought

The only way to keep your health is to eat what you don't want, drink what you don't like, and do what you'd rather not.

—MARK TWAIN, humorist and writer

Tell me what you eat, and I shall tell you what you are.

—JEAN ANTHELME BRILLAT-SAVARIN, gastronome, philosopher, and writer

Eating is touch carried to the bitter end.

—SAMUEL BUTLER, writer

An idealist is one who, on noticing that a rose smells better than a cabbage, concludes that it will also make a better soup.

—H. L. MENCKEN, journalist

The next time you feel like complaining, remember that your garbage disposal probably eats better than 30 percent of the people in the world.

—ROBERT ORBEN, comedy writer

Aïoli (garlic mayonnaise) epitomizes the heat, the power, and the joy of the Provençal sun, but it has another virtue—it drives away flies.

—FRÉDÉRIC MISTRAL, poet

Tomatoes and oregano make it Italian; wine and tarragon make it French. Sour cream makes it Russian; lemon and cinnamon make it Greek. Soy sauce makes it Chinese; garlic makes it good.

—ALICE MAY BROCK, illustrator and writer

Don't eat too many almonds; they add weight to the breasts.

—COLETTE, writer

An apple is an excellent thing—until you have tried a peach.

—GEORGE DU MAURIER, illustrator and novelist

These things are just plain annoying. After all the trouble you go to, you get about as much actual food out of eating an artichoke as you would from licking thirty or forty postage stamps. Have the shrimp cocktail instead.

—MISS PIGGY, Muppet

The rich would have to eat money if the poor did not provide food.

—RUSSIAN PROVERB

How can you govern a country which has 246 varieties of cheese?

—CHARLES DE GAULLE, French general and statesman

Bread is like dresses, hats, and shoes—in other words, essential!

—EMILY POST, etiquette expert and writer

I refuse to believe that trading recipes is silly. Tuna-fish casserole is at least as real as corporate stock.

—BARBARA GRIZZUTI HARRISON, writer

A kitchen without a lemon is like a song without a tune.

—DAVID WHEELER, writer

If I ever had to practice cannibalism, I might manage if there were enough tarragon around.

—James Beard, chef

There are some things that sound too funny to eat—guacamole. That sounds like something you yell when you're on fire.

—George Carlin, comedian

As one of the kids rummaged in the refrigerator, he said, "What's this?"
"It's celery and it's good for you."
He said, "If it's so great, then how come it never danced on television?"
I couldn't answer him.

—Erma Bombeck, columnist and writer

The best sauce in the world is hunger.

—MIGUEL DE CERVANTES, writer

There is no such thing as bad bread when you have a good appetite.

—GABRIEL GARCÍA MÁRQUEZ, writer

In the Lord's Prayer, the first petition is for daily bread. No one can worship God or love his neighbor on an empty stomach.

—WOODROW WILSON, U.S. president

To a man with an empty stomach, food is God.

—MAHATMA GANDHI, spiritual and political leader

Everything you see I owe to spaghetti.

—SOPHIA LOREN, actress

Things taste better in small houses.

—VICTORIA, queen of England

If toast always lands butter side down and cats always land on their feet, what happens if you strap toast on the back of a cat and drop it?

—STEVEN WRIGHT, comedian

What's Cooking?

Happy and successful cooking doesn't rely only on know-how; it comes from the heart, makes great demands on the palate, and needs enthusiasm and a deep love of food to bring it to life.

—GEORGES BLANC, chef and writer

I like a cook who smiles out loud when he tastes his own work. Let God worry about your modesty; I want to see your enthusiasm.

—ROBERT FARRAR CAPON, priest, chef, and writer

Good painting is like good cooking; it can be tasted, but not explained.

—MAURICE DE VLAMINCK, Fauvist painter

Good cooking does not depend on whether the dish is large or small, expensive or economical. If one has the art, then a piece of celery or salted cabbage can be made into a marvelous delicacy; whereas if one has not the art, not all the greatest delicacies and rarities of land, sea, or sky are of any avail.

—YUAN MEI, eighteenth-century poet

The preparation of good food is merely another expression of art, one of the joys of civilized living.

—DIONE LUCAS, chef

My kitchen is a mystical place, a kind of temple for me. It is a place where the surfaces seem to have significance, where the sounds and odors carry meaning that transfers from the past and bridges to the future.

—PEARL BAILEY, singer and actress

A good meal must be as harmonious as a symphony and as well constructed as a Norman cathedral.

—FERNAND POINT, restaurateur and writer

To give life to beauty, the painter uses a whole range of colors; musicians of sounds; the cook of tastes—and it is indeed remarkable that there are seven colors, seven musical notes, and seven tastes.

—LUCIEN TENDRET, lawyer and gastronome

Cooking is at once child's play and adult joy. And cooking done with care is an act of love.

—CRAIG CLAIBORNE, culinary writer

Don't take a butcher's advice on how to cook meat. If he knew, he'd be a chef.

—ANDY ROONEY,
journalist and television personality

There is no technique; there is just the way to do it. Now, are we going to measure or are we going to cook?

—FRANCES MAYES, chef and writer

Carve a ham as if you were shaving the face of a friend.

—HENRI CHARPENTIER, chef and writer

No artist can work simply for results; he must also *like* the work of getting them.... If a man has never been pleasantly surprised at the way the custard sets or flour thickens, there is not much hope of making a cook of him.

—ROBERT FARRAR CAPON, priest, chef, and writer

The dangerous person in the kitchen is the one who goes rigidly by weights, measurements, thermometers, and scales.

—X. Marcel Boulestin, chef and culinary writer

Cooking is a great form of stress relief.

—Queen Latifah, rapper and actress

What I love about cooking is that, after a hard day, there is something comforting about the fact that if you melt butter and add flour and then hot stock, *it will get thick!* It's a sure thing! It's a sure thing in a world where nothing is sure; it has a mathematical certainty in a world where those of us who long for some kind of certainty are forced to settle for crossword puzzles.

—Nora Ephron, writer

Everyone has the talent to some degree; even making a peanut butter and jelly sandwich, you know whether it tastes better to you with raspberry jam or grape jelly, on chewy pumpernickel or white toast.

—ANNA SHAPIRO, chef and writer

I feel a recipe is only a theme, which an intelligent cook can play each time with a variation.

—MADAME BENOIT, chef and writer

'Tis an ill cook that cannot lick his own fingers.

—WILLIAM SHAKESPEARE,
playwright, *Romeo and Juliet*

Noncooks think it's silly to invest two hours' work in two minutes' enjoyment, but if cooking is evanescent, well, so is ballet.

—JULIA CHILD, chef

Some people's food always tastes better than others', even if they are cooking the same dish at the same dinner. Now I will tell you why: because one person has more life in them—more fire, more vitality, more guts—than others. A person without these things can never make food taste right; no matter what materials you give them, it is no use.

—ROSA LEWIS, chef

Our lives are not in the lap of the gods, but in the lap of our cooks.

—LIN YUTANG, linguist, philosopher, and writer

A good cook is like a sorceress who dispenses happiness.

—ELSA SCHIAPARELLI, designer

Go into the kitchen to shake the chef's hand. If he is thin, have second thoughts about eating there; if he is thin and sad, flee.

—FERNAND POINT, *New York Times* food critic

Once learnt, this business of cooking was to prove an ever-growing burden. It scarcely bears thinking about, the time and labour that man-and woman-kind has devoted to the preparation of dishes that are to melt and vanish in a moment like smoke or a dream, like a shadow, and as a post that hastes by, and the air closes behind them, afterwards no sign where they went is to be found.

—ROSE MACAULAY, writer

"And please don't cook me, kind sirs! I am a good cook myself, and cook better than I cook, if you know what I mean. I'll cook beautifully for you, a perfectly beautiful breakfast for you, if only you won't have me for supper."

—BILBO BAGGINS, to the Trolls in
J. R. R. Tolkien's *The Hobbit*

Too many cooks spoil the broth.

—ENGLISH PROVERB

The fricassee with dumplings is made by a Mrs. Miller, whose husband has left her four times on account of her disposition and returned four times on account of her cooking and is still there.

—REX STOUT, mystery writer

No mean woman can cook well, for it calls for a light head, a generous spirit, and a large heart.

—PAUL GAUGUIN, artist

It is odd how all men develop the notion, as they grow older, that their mothers were wonderful cooks. I have yet to meet a man who will admit that his mother was a kitchen assassin and nearly poisoned him.

—ROBERTSON DAVIES, writer

There is one thing more exasperating than a wife who can cook and won't, and that's a wife who can't cook and will.

—ROBERT FROST, poet

In cooking, as in all the arts, simplicity is the sign of perfection.

—CURNONSKY, gastronome and writer

If you are lazy and dump everything together, they won't come out as well as if you add one thing at a time. It's like everything else—no shortcuts without compromising quality.

—LIONEL POIL,NE, baker

Kissing don't last: cookery do.

—GEORGE MEREDITH, poet

Even an old boot tastes good if it is cooked over charcoal.

—ITALIAN FOLK PROVERB

The secret to good cooking resides in the cook's ability to say "the hell with the basic recipe" and improvise freely from it. If you haven't got this kind of moxie, you might as well hang up your apron.

—JAMES ALAN MCPHERSON, writer

Food that's beautiful to look at seems to taste better than food that isn't.

—EMERIL LAGASSE, chef and writer

Cooking is like love. It should be entered into with abandon or not at all.

—HARRIET VAN HORNE, newspaper columnist

When we decode a cookbook, every one of us is a practicing chemist. Cooking is really the oldest, most basic application of physical and chemical forces to natural materials.

—ARTHUR E. GROSSER, Professor of Chemistry

I never see any home cooking. All I get is fancy stuff.

—PRINCE PHILIP, DUKE OF EDINBURGH

I don't like gourmet cooking or "this" cooking or "that" cooking. I like good cooking.

—JAMES BEARD, chef

Let Them Eat Really Good Cake

Actually, the true gourmet, like the true artist, is one of the unhappiest creatures existent. His trouble comes from so seldom finding what he constantly seeks: perfection.

—LUDWIG BEMELMANS, children's writer

A gourmet is a being pleasing to the heavens.

—CHARLES PIERRE MONSELET, writer

A gourmet who thinks of calories is like a tart who looks at her watch.

—JAMES BEARD, chef

For a gourmet, wine is not a drink but a condiment, provided that your host has chosen correctly.

—EDOUARD DE POMAINE, writer

Tastes are made, not born.

—MARK TWAIN, humorist and writer

Smell and taste are in fact but a single composite sense, whose laboratory is the mouth and its chimney the nose.

—JEAN ANTHELME BRILLAT-SAVARIN,
gastronome, philosopher, and writer

The quality of food is in inverse proportion to the altitude of the dining room, with airplanes the extreme example.

—BRYAN MILLER, *New York Times* food critic

To me, an airplane is a great place to diet.

—WOLFGANG PUCK, chef and restaurateur

You needn't tell me that a man who doesn't love oysters and asparagus and good wines has got a soul, or a stomach either. He's simply got the instinct for being unhappy.

—SAKI (A.K.A. HECTOR HUGH MUNRO), writer

An epicure is one who gets nothing better than the cream of everything but cheerfully makes the best of it.

—OLIVER HERFORD,
illustrator, comedian, poet, and writer

One only dines well at the homes of true gastronomes who feel all the nuances; the least puffiness spoils the loveliest of faces, and attention to detail creates perfection.

—LUCIEN TENDRET, lawyer and gastronome

The gastronome is at the same time inquisitive and timid; he explores faintheartedly. He spends half his time remembering past satisfactions and the other half skeptically calculating future possibilities.

—J. F. REVEL, philosopher and writer,
Un Festin en Paroles

Health food makes me sick.

—CALVIN TRILLIN, writer

Talking of Pleasure, this moment I was writing with one hand, and with the other holding to my Mouth a Nectarine—how good how fine. It went down all pulpy, slushy, oozy—all its delicious embonpoint melted down my throat like a large, beatified Strawberry.

—JOHN KEATS, poet

Caviar is to dining what a sable coat is to a girl in evening.

—LUDWIG BEMELMANS, children's writer

My idea of heaven is eating pâtés de foie gras to the sound of trumpets.

—SYDNEY SMITH, essayist

A few limpid slivers of moist and milky veal, spun round with a tracing of succulent sauce, accented with a few perfect ovals of baby carrot, a graceful arch of herb. Each mouthful is so poignant, however, that our appetite, if not assuaged, is at last abashed. To be hungry before such food is as vulgar—as seemingly wrong as feeling lust before the Venus de Milo.

—JOHN THORNE, culinary writer

The olive tree is surely the richest gift of Heaven. I can scarcely expect bread.

—THOMAS JEFFERSON, U.S. president

While an eon, as someone has observed, may be two people and a ham, a fruitcake is forever.

—RUSSELL BAKER, writer

Never eat at a place called Mom's.

—NELSON ALGREN, writer

Another good appetizer is stewed white mushrooms, with onion, you know, and bay leaf and other spices. You lift the lid off the dish, and the steam rises, a smell of mushrooms…sometimes it really brings tears to my eyes.

—ANTON CHEKHOV, writer

It requires a certain kind of mind to see beauty in a hamburger bun.

—Ray Kroc, founder of McDonald's

Presently we were aware of an odour gradually coming towards us, something musky, fiery, savoury, mysterious—a hot, drowsy smell that lulls the senses and yet enflames them—the truffles were coming.

—W. M. Thackeray, writer

Those from whom nature has withheld taste invented trousers.

—Jean Anthelme Brillat-Savarin, gastronome, philosopher, and writer

Peanut butter—the pâté of childhood.

—Florence Fabricant, culinary writer

Clean Plate Club

He who distinguishes the true savor of his food can never be a glutton; he who does not cannot be otherwise.

—HENRY DAVID THOREAU, writer

I am not a glutton—I am an explorer of food.

—ERMA BOMBECK, columnist and writer

A true gastronome should always be ready to eat, just as a soldier should always be ready to fight.

—CHARLES PIERRE MONSELET, writer

Gluttony is an emotional escape, a sign that something is eating us.

—PETER DE VRIES, screenwriter

Gluttony is a great fault, but we do not necessarily dislike a glutton. We only dislike the glutton when he becomes a gourmet—that is, we only dislike him when he not only wants the best for himself, but knows what is best for other people.

—G. K. CHESTERTON, debater and writer

You first parents of the human race...who ruined yourself for an apple, what might you have done for a truffled turkey?

—JEAN ANTHELME BRILLAT-SAVARIN, gastronome, philosopher, and writer

I have eaten my way through six inheritances in the great restaurants, so I know what good cuisine is all about.

—DENIS (LAHANA DENIS), chef, restaurateur, and writer

Nature will castigate those who don't masticate.

—HORACE FLETCHER (A.K.A. THE GREAT MASTICATOR),
diet guru and writer

All knives and forks were working away at a rate that was quite alarming; very few words were spoken, and everybody seemed to eat his utmost, in self defense, as if a famine were expected to set in before breakfast-time to-morrow morning, and it had become high time to assert the first law of nature.

—CHARLES DICKENS, writer, *Martin Chuzzlewit*

Gluttony, it is to thee we owe our griefs!

—GEOFFREY CHAUCER, writer

My fare is really sumptuous this evening: buffaloes' humps, tongues and marrowbones, fine trout, parched meal, pepper and salt, and a good appetite; the last is not considered the least of the luxuries.

—From *The Journals of Lewis and Clark*,
Thursday, June 13, 1805

Don't eat until you're full; eat until you're tired!

—HAWAIIAN PROVERB

A gourmet is just a glutton with brains.

—PHILIP W. HABERMAN JR.,
from "How to Be a Calorie Chisler," *Vogue*, 1961

The glutton digs his grave with his teeth.

—ENGLISH PROVERB

I eat merely to put food out of my mind.

—N. F. SIMPSON, writer

My doctor told me to stop having intimate dinners for four. Unless there are three other people.

—ORSON WELLES, actor, director, and writer

The way one eats on a diet is the way people in famine think about food—obsessively, with great care—but turned upside down.

—SALLIE TISDALE, editor and writer,
The Best Thing I Ever Tasted

He who eats for two must work for three.

—KURDISH PROVERB

In general, mankind since the improvement of cookery eats twice as much as nature requires.

—BENJAMIN FRANKLIN, inventor, statesman, and writer

It is a hard matter, my fellow citizens, to argue with the belly since it has no ears.

—PLUTARCH, Greek biographer and essayist

What drives you to make dolmades, a dish that requires hours and disappears in minutes? Like the power of a curse lifted—anyone who has ever tasted it is subject to an occasional greed and hunger that nothing else can satisfy.... Each one swallowed creates the need for another, an anxiety that there will not be enough. Since hours have been spent by not one cook but many, there is nothing to stop you from eating until you feel your stomach might burst.

—CATHERINE TEMMA DAVIDSON,
writer, *The Priest Fainted*

'Tis not the meat, but the appetite makes eating a delight.

—Sir John Suckling, poet

Peter was ill during the evening, on consequence of overeating himself. His mother put him to bed and gave him a dose of chamomile tea, but Flopsy, Mopsy, and Cottontail had bread and milk and blackberries for supper.

—Beatrix Potter, children's writer

Vegetables are a must on any diet. I suggest carrot cake, zucchini bread, and pumpkin pie.

—Garfield, cartoon cat

Indigestion is charged by God with enforcing morality on the stomach.

—Victor Hugo, writer

Never eat more than you can lift.

—MISS PIGGY, Muppet

Life itself is the proper binge.

—JULIA CHILD, chef

In the lexicon of lip-smacking, an *epicure* is fastidious in his choice and enjoyment of food, just a soupçon more expert than a *gastronome*; a *gourmet* is a connoisseur of the exotic, taste buds attuned to the calibrations of deliciousness, who savors the masterly techniques of great chefs; a *gourmand* is a hearty bon vivant who enjoys food without truffles and flourishes; a *glutton* overindulges greedily, the word rooted in the Latin for "one who devours."

—WILLIAM SAFIRE, journalist and speechwriter

My regimen is lust and avarice for exercise, gluttony and sloth for relaxation.

—MASON COOLEY, aphorist

God forgives the sin of gluttony.

—CATALAN PROVERB

In love, as in gluttony, pleasure is a matter of the utmost precision.

—ITALO CALVINO, writer and critic

Drink Up!

A man hath no better thing under the sun than to eat, and to drink, and to be merry.

—Ecclesiastes 8:15

Eat with the fingers, drink with the nose.

—Joseph Delteil, writer

Let me fix you a martini that's pure magic. It may not make life's problems disappear, but it'll certainly reduce their size.

—From the 1959 film *Some Came Running*, starring Frank Sinatra and Dean Martin

Wine is sunlight, held together by water.

—Galileo Galilei, astronomer and mathematician

You can no more keep a martini in the refrigerator than you can keep a kiss there. The proper union of gin and vermouth is...one of the happiest marriages on earth, and one of the shortest lived.

—BERNARD DE VOTO, writer

The problem with the world is that everyone is a few drinks behind.

—HUMPHREY BOGART, actor

I love to drink martinis
Two at the very most
Three I'm under the table
Four I'm under the host.

—DOROTHY PARKER, writer

Beer is proof that God loves us and wants us to be happy.

—BENJAMIN FRANKLIN,
inventor, statesman, and writer

Champagne's funny stuff. I'm used to whiskey. Whiskey is a slap on the back, and champagne's a heavy mist before my eyes.

—JAMES STEWART, actor

If you ever reach total enlightenment while drinking beer, I bet it makes beer shoot out your nose.

—From "DEEP THOUGHTS BY JACK HANDEY,"
on *Saturday Night Live*

Without question, the greatest invention in the history of mankind is beer. Oh, I grant you that the wheel was also a fine invention, but the wheel does not go nearly as well with pizza.

—DAVE BARRY, comedian and writer

I would kill everyone in this room for a drop of sweet beer.

—HOMER SIMPSON,
cartoon character and Duff beer lover

There comes a time in every woman's life when the only thing that helps is a glass of champagne.

—BETTE DAVIS, actress, in *Old Acquaintance*

Beer does not make itself properly, by itself. It takes an element of mystery, and of things that no one can understand.

—FRITZ MAYTAG,
Anchor Brewing Company president

No, sir: There is nothing which has yet been contrived by man by which so much happiness is produced as by a good tavern or inn.

—SAMUEL JOHNSON, writer

A meal without wine is like a day without sunshine.

—JEAN ANTHELME BRILLAT-SAVARIN,
gastronome, philosopher, and writer

So, when he looked down into his martini, he was put into a trance by dancing myriads of winking eyes on the surface of his drink. The eyes were beads of lemon oil.

—KURT VONNEGUT JR., writer,
Breakfast of Champions

Wine makes a symphony of a good meal.

—FERNANDE GARVIN, chef and writer

Wine has a drastic, an astringent taste. I cannot help wincing as I drink. Ascent of flowers, radiance and heat, are distilled here to a fiery, yellow liquid. Just behind my shoulder blades some dry thing, wide-eyed, gently closes, gradually lulls itself to sleep. This is rapture. This is relief.

—VIRGINIA WOOLF, writer

In Europe we thought of wine as something as healthy and normal as food and also a great giver of happiness and well-being and delight. Drinking wine was not a snobbism nor a sign of sophistication nor a cult; it was as natural as eating and to me as necessary.

—ERNEST HEMINGWAY, expatriate and writer

Quaintest thoughts, queerest fancies come to life and fade away. What care I how time advances; I am drinking ale today.

—EDGAR ALLAN POE, writer

Do not cease to drink beer, to eat, to intoxicate thyself, to make love, and to celebrate the good days.

—ANCIENT EGYPTIAN PROVERB

Wine is bottled poetry.

—ROBERT LOUIS STEVENSON, writer

A man's got to believe in something. I believe I'll have another drink.

—W. C. FIELDS, comedian and actor

A drink a day keeps the shrink away.

—EDWARD ABBEY, writer

If the Lord hadn't intended to have a three martini lunch, then why do you suppose he put all those olive trees in the Holy Land?

—JIM WRIGHT, U.S. congressman and Speaker of the House of Representatives

Coffee should be black as hell, strong as death, and sweet as love.

—TURKISH PROVERB

Abstainer: a weak person who yields to the temptation of denying himself a pleasure.

—AMBROSE BIERCE, writer

Come quickly, I am tasting the stars!

—DOM PERIGNON, champagne maker,
upon first discovering champagne

For Sweets' Sake

The only emperor is the emperor of ice cream.

—WALLACE STEVENS, poet

A house is beautiful not because of its walls, but because of its cakes.

—OLD RUSSIAN PROVERB

I would stand transfixed before the windows of the confectioners' shops, fascinated by the luminous sparkle of candied fruits: the cloudy luster of jellies, the kaleidoscope inflorescence of acidulated fruit drops—red, green, orange, violet; I coveted the colours themselves as much as the pleasure they promised me. Mama used to grind sugared almonds for me in a mortar and mix the crunched powder with a yellow cream; the pink of the sweets used to shade off into exquisite nuances of colour, and I would dip an eager spoon into their brilliant sunset.

—SIMONE DE BEAUVOIR, feminist and writer

Had I but a penny in the world, thou shouldst have it for gingerbread.

—WILLIAM SHAKESPEARE, playwright

Oh, blackberry tart, with berries as big as your thumb, purple and black, and thick with juice, and a crust to endear them that will go to cream in your mouth, and both passing down with such a taste that will make you close your eyes and wish you might live forever in the wideness of that rich moment.

—RICHARD LLEWELLYN, writer

Health may be good for the conscience, but Oreos taste a hell of a lot better.

—ROBERT REDFORD, actor

Few pleasures are greater than turning out a perfect cake.... Such creations can bring happiness to both our childhood and mature years, for few, if any people are immune to their charm, and memories of them...lighten the dark corners of life.

—JOSEPH AMENDOLA AND DONALD E. LUNDBERG,
coauthors

I doubt whether the world holds for anyone a more soul-stirring surprise than the first adventure with ice cream.

—HEYWOOD BROUN, journalist

That year I discovered the secret of every experienced cook: desserts are a cheap trick. People love them even when they're bad. And so I began to bake, appreciating the alchemy that can turn flour, water, chocolate, and butter into devil's food cake and make it disappear in a flash.

—RUTH REICHL, chef and writer

A dessert without cheese is like a beautiful woman with only one eye.

—JEAN ANTHELME BRILLAT-SAVARIN,
gastronome, philosopher, and writer

The only reason for a bee that I know of is making honey…and the only reason for making honey is so I can eat it.

—WINNIE THE POOH,
beloved bear and honey connoisseur

Fancy is as fancy does, and nothing could be fancier than little fruit tartlets.

—JENNIFER PATERSON, chef and coauthor,
The Two Fat Ladies Ride Again

I adore seafood, especially saltwater taffy.

—MILTON BERLE, comedian and actor

'Yes,' said Frog, reaching for a cookie, 'we need will power.'

'What is will power?' asked Toad.

'Will power is trying hard not to do something you really want to do,' said Frog.

'You mean like trying not to eat all of these cookies?' asked Toad.

'Right,' said Frog.

—FROG AND TOAD, friends, from Arnold Lobel's
The Adventures of Frog and Toad

When there's no opportunity for anything erotic, a handful of Hershey's kisses is the next best thing.

—PETER GALLAGHER, singer and actor

A Georgia peach, a real Georgia peach, a backyard great-grandmother's orchard peach, is as thickly furred as a sweater, and so fluent and sweet that once you bite through the flannel, it brings tears to your eyes.

—MELISSA FAY GREENE, writer, *Praying for Sheetrock*

What is a roofless cathedral compared to a well-built pie?

—WILLIAM MAGINN, writer

Good apple pies are a considerable part of our domestic happiness.

—JANE AUSTEN, writer

Animal crackers, and cocoa to drink
That is the finest of suppers, I think
When I'm grown up and can have what I please,
I think I shall always insist upon these.

—CHRISTOPHER MORLEY,
founder of the *Saturday Review*

Life is like a box of chocolates. You never know
what you're going to get.

—TOM HANKS, actor, in *Forrest Gump*

Eat Your
Heart Out

The most indispensable ingredient of all good home cooking: love for those you are cooking for.

—SOPHIA LOREN, actress

My idea of heaven is a great big baked potato and someone to share it with.

—OPRAH WINFREY, media mogul

For those who love it, cooking is at once child's play and adult joy. And cooking done with care is an act of love.

—CRAIG CLAIBORNE, culinary writer

Sex is good, but not as fresh sweet corn.

—GARRISON KEILLOR, writer

The way to a man's heart is through his stomach.

—Fanny Fern, writer

That's the way Chinese mothers show they love their children, not through hugs and kisses, but with stern offerings of steamed dumplings, duck's gizzards, and crab.

—Amy Tan, writer, *The Joy Luck Club*

Nothing takes the taste out of peanut butter quite like unrequited love.

—Charlie Brown, cartoon character

I've always seen that food and passion are synonymous.

—Harvey Weinstein, movie producer

Her breath is like honey spiced with cloves,
Her mouth delicious as a ripened mango.

—KUMARADADATTA,
twelfth-century poet, *Srngarakarika*

A plenteous meal may produce voluptuous sensations.

—MARQUIS DE SADE, writer

Love doesn't just sit there, like a stone; it has to be made, like bread, remade all the time, made new.

—URSULA K. LE GUIN, writer

I'm at the age where food has taken the place of sex in my life. In fact, I've just had a mirror put over my kitchen table.

—RODNEY DANGERFIELD, comedian and actor

I cannot separate eroticism from food and see no reason to do so. On the contrary, I want to go on enjoying both as long as strength and good humor last.

—Isabel Allende, writer

There is no sight on earth more appealing than the sight of a woman making dinner for someone she loves.

—Thomas Wolfe, writer

Comfort me with apples: for I am sick of love.

—Song of Solomon 2:4

Anyone who eats three meals a day should under-stand why cookbooks outsell sex books, three to one.

—L. M. BOYD, newspaper columnist